HAPPY HAUNTING!
HALLOWEEN COSTUMES
YOU CAN MAKE

Written by Judith Conaway
Illustrated by Renzo Barto

Troll Associates

Library of Congress Cataloging in Publication Data

Conaway, Judith, (date)
 Happy haunting.

 Summary: Instructions for making Halloween costumes
such as ghost, pirate, and goblin and accompanying
necessities such as rattling chains, tattoos, Bigfoot
tracks, and a variety of masks.
 1. Costume—Juvenile literature. 2. Halloween—
Juvenile literature. [1. Costume. 2. Halloween]
I. Barto, Renzo, ill. II. Title.
TT633.C65   1986   745.5   85-28840
ISBN 0-8167-0666-2 (lib. bdg.)
ISBN 0-8167-0667-0 (pbk.)

CONTENTS

BASIC SHEET GHOST
Here's what you need:

Old white sheet

Crayons or markers

Scissors

Here's what you do:

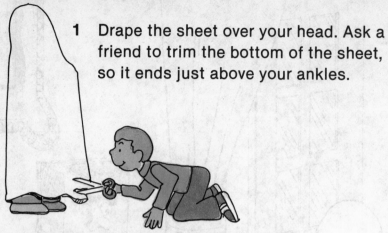

1 Drape the sheet over your head. Ask a friend to trim the bottom of the sheet, so it ends just above your ankles.

2 Now make eyeholes. Have your friend put a hand on your head, to keep the sheet from sliding. Bring your hands outside the sheet and up to your face.

3 Very lightly, using a marker or crayon, mark a dot where each eye is. Take the sheet off and draw circles around the marks you made. Cut out the circles.

4 You may also want to cut holes for your arms. To do this, put the sheet over your head with the eyeholes in place. Hold your arms out in front of you. Have your friend mark the two places where your hands will come out. Remove the sheet and cut the holes.

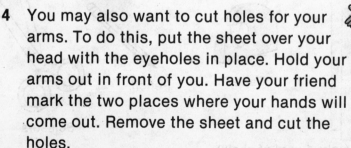

RATTLING CHAINS

Don't get rattled! It's only a ghost! Here's how you can make chain necklaces and belts to go with your ghost costume. You might also want to hang up these chains at your next ghostly gathering.

Here's what you need:

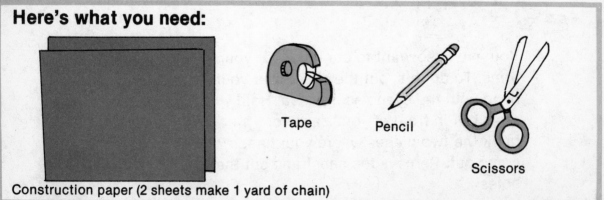

Tape

Pencil

Scissors

Construction paper (2 sheets make 1 yard of chain)

Here's what you do:

1 Fold a sheet of paper in half, then cut along the fold. Fold each half in half... and in half again.

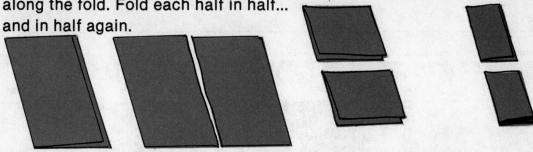

2 Unfold all the paper. Cut the rectangles apart. You will get 8 rectangles from 1 full sheet of paper. Each rectangle makes a link in the chain.

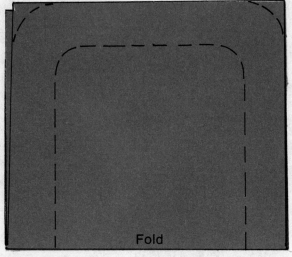

Fold

3 To make a link, fold a rectangle in half, like this. Copy this pattern on the paper. Carefully cut out the link.

4 Tape the open end of the first link closed. To thread the chain, keep the links folded. Pass the folded end of one link through both folded ends of another link.

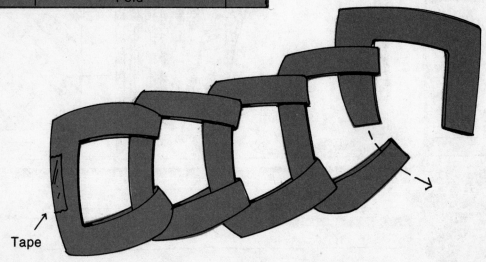

Tape

GHOSTLY GRAB BAG

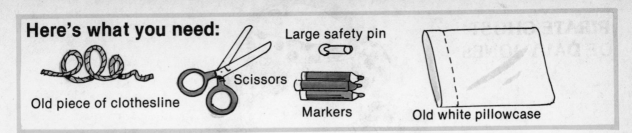

Here's what you need:

Old piece of clothesline

Scissors

Large safety pin

Markers

Old white pillowcase

Here's what you do:

1 Cut a slit in the hem of a pillowcase.

2 Make a knot in one end of the clothesline. Pin a large safety pin to the knot.

3 Using the safety pin as a small handle, push the clothesline through the hole in the hem of the pillowcase. The clothesline should go all around the hem and come out the same hole.

4 Remove the safety pin and tie the two ends of the clothesline together.

5 Then tie a double knot in front of the slit, to form a loop handle. To close the bag, just pull the rope. Use markers to decorate the bag with Halloween designs.

PIRATE GHOST
OF DAVY JONES

Here's what you need:

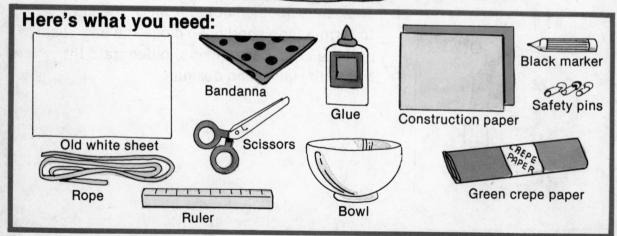

Old white sheet

Bandanna

Glue

Construction paper

Black marker

Safety pins

Rope

Scissors

Ruler

Bowl

Green crepe paper

CREPE
PAPER

Here's what you do:

1 Start by making the sheet ghost shown on page 4. Use a black marker to draw a skull and crossbones—or other pirate designs—on the sheet.

2 Make seaweed out of green crepe paper. Start with a roll of folded paper. Cut thin strips across the folds. The strips should be about ½ inch wide.

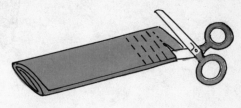

3 Unfold the strips and lay them out in long bundles. Tie each bundle around the middle with a strip of crepe paper.

4 Dip each bundle of paper strips into a bowl of water. Hang the bundles up to dry. When dry, they will fade and crinkle like seaweed.

5 Cut seashell shapes or starfish out of construction paper. Glue them to your costume. Then use safety pins to attach clumps of seaweed to the sheet.

6 Now you're ready to get dressed. Put on your ghostly sheet. Tie the bandanna around your head. Drape an old rope across your chest.

Want to make Davy Jones even more ghostly? On the following pages you'll find instructions for making pirate tattoos, a pirate's eye patch, and even a parrot puppet!

PIRATE TATTOOS

Here's what you need:

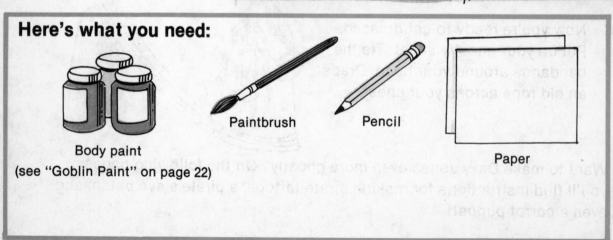

Paintbrush

Pencil

Paper

Body paint
(see "Goblin Paint" on page 22)

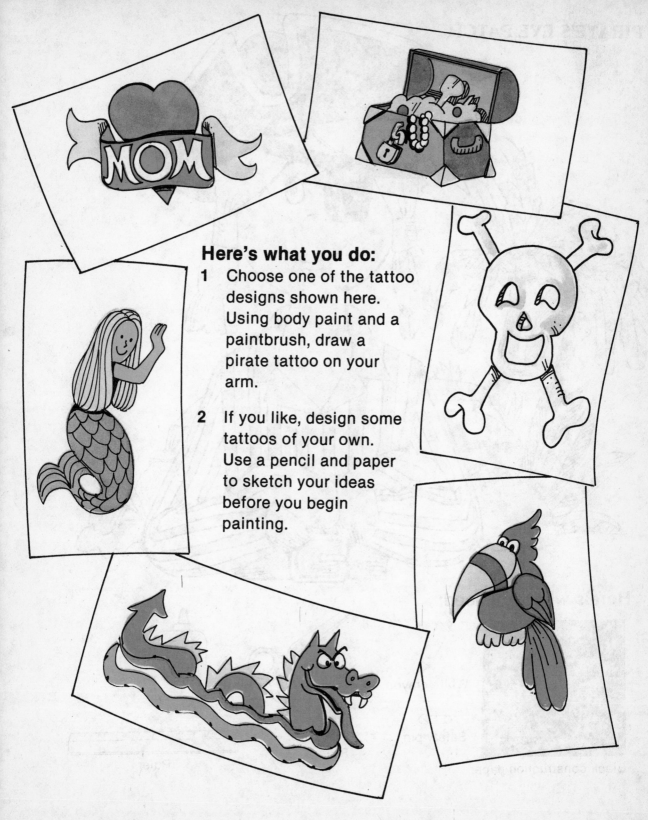

Here's what you do:

1 Choose one of the tattoo designs shown here. Using body paint and a paintbrush, draw a pirate tattoo on your arm.

2 If you like, design some tattoos of your own. Use a pencil and paper to sketch your ideas before you begin painting.

PIRATE'S EYE PATCH

Here's what you need:

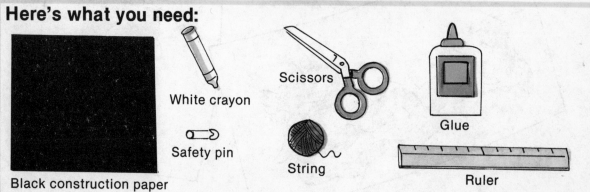

Black construction paper

White crayon

Safety pin

Scissors

String

Glue

Ruler

Here's what you do:

1 Using white crayon, draw the patch shape shown below onto black paper.

2 Cut out the eye patch. Then cut out 3 or 4 strips of black paper. Each strip should be 1 inch wide by 8 inches long.

3 Use a string to measure the distance around your head, where the band will go.

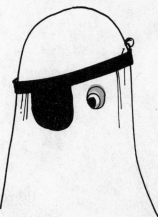

4 Glue the strips together so they are an inch longer than the string.

5 Glue the eye patch to one end of the strip. Then glue the strip closed in a loop.

6 To wear the eye patch with the ghost outfit, first put on the sheet. Slip the band of the eye patch over your head, making sure the eye patch covers one eye. Then ask an adult to help you pin the band to the sheet with a safety pin. (If you're wearing a pirate costume, the eye patch will also come in handy!)

DAVY JONES' GHOSTLY PARROT PUPPET

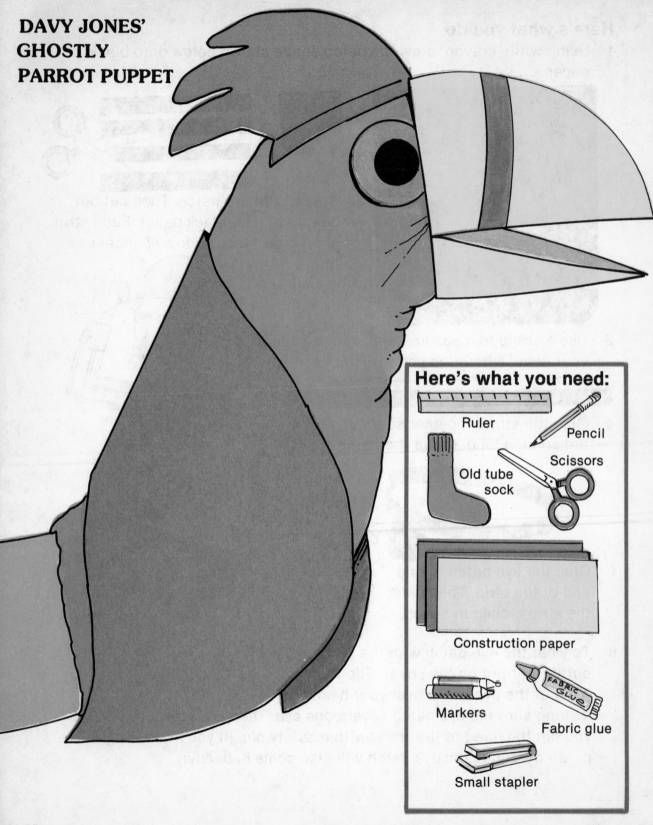

Here's what you need:

Ruler

Pencil

Old tube sock

Scissors

Construction paper

Markers

FABRIC GLUE

Fabric glue

Small stapler

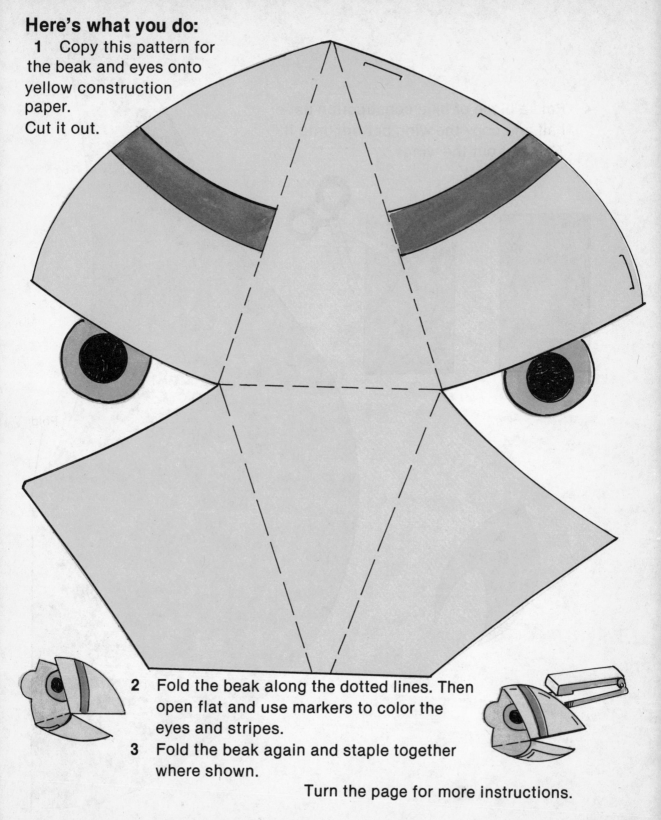

Here's what you do:

1 Copy this pattern for the beak and eyes onto yellow construction paper.
Cut it out.

2 Fold the beak along the dotted lines. Then open flat and use markers to color the eyes and stripes.

3 Fold the beak again and staple together where shown.

Turn the page for more instructions.

4 Fold a piece of blue construction paper in half and copy the wing pattern onto it. Then cut out the wings.

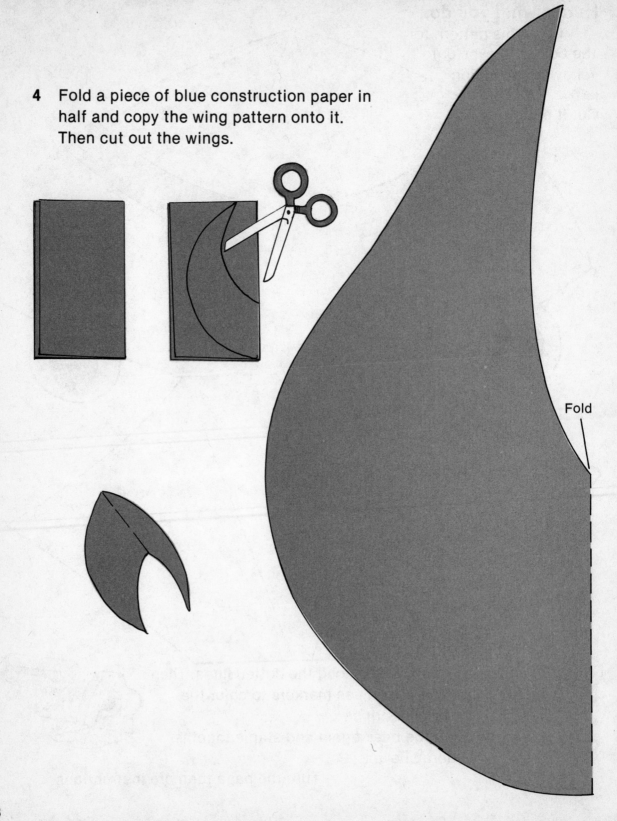

Fold

5 Use this pattern for the head feathers. Copy it onto red construction paper. Then cut it out. Fold along dotted lines where shown. Then glue the sections together to form an upside-down V, as shown. Allow to dry.

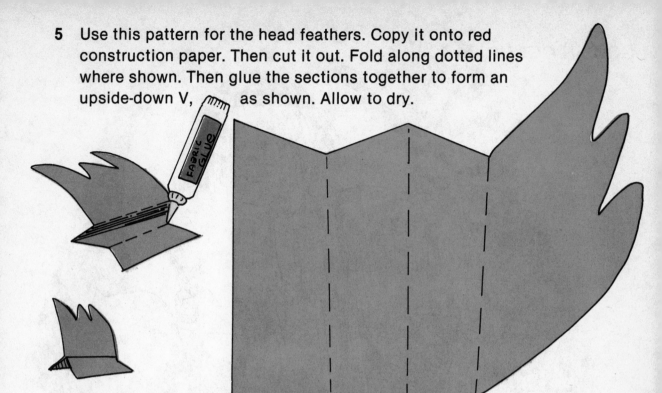

6 To put the parrot together, pull the sock over your hand so that your thumb pushes into the heel of the sock. Your fingers should stretch into the toe area. Apply fabric glue to the outside of the sock where the beak will go. Fit the beak in place.

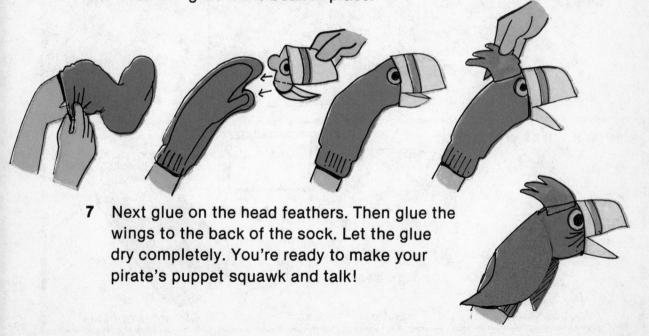

7 Next glue on the head feathers. Then glue the wings to the back of the sock. Let the glue dry completely. You're ready to make your pirate's puppet squawk and talk!

GOBLIN GET-UP

Here's what you need:

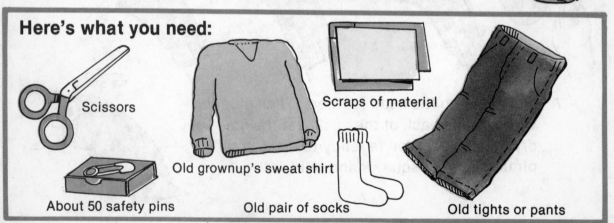

Scissors

Scraps of material

Old grownup's sweat shirt

Old pair of socks

Old tights or pants

About 50 safety pins

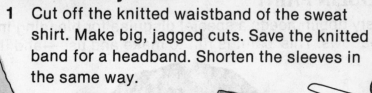

Here's what you do:

1 Cut off the knitted waistband of the sweat shirt. Make big, jagged cuts. Save the knitted band for a headband. Shorten the sleeves in the same way.

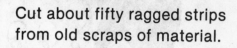

2 Cut about fifty ragged strips from old scraps of material.

3 Use safety pins to attach the strips to the sweat shirt. Pin some of the strips to a pair of old socks.

4 Now cut a headband from the knitted band of the sweat shirt. It should be long enough to fit around your head, with about 6 inches of extra material. Pin strips of material to the headband to give yourself ragged goblin hair.

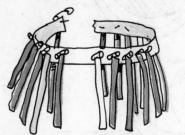

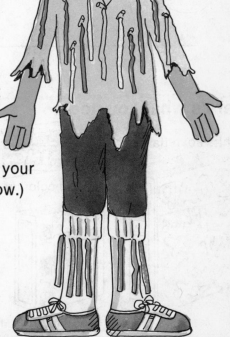

5 To put your goblin costume together, put on the socks and pull them up over the pants. You're ready for some goblin fun!

(If you'd like to add some Goblin Paint to your costume, just turn the page to find out how.)

GOBLIN PAINT

Every goblin needs a special disguise for blending into the fields and meadows. This paint is fun to make and use—and it's washable!

Here's what you need:

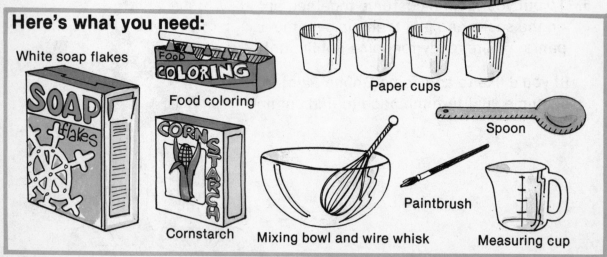

White soap flakes

Food coloring

Cornstarch

Paper cups

Spoon

Mixing bowl and wire whisk

Paintbrush

Measuring cup

Here's what you do:

1 Pour 1 cup of soap flakes and ½ cup of warm water into a bowl. Beat the mixture with a wire whisk until it is foamy.

Soap flakes

Warm water

Here are some ideas for your goblin disguise.

2 While stirring the mixture, add cornstarch, a pinch at a time, until the mixture is thick.

3 Pour the mixture into paper cups. Use one cup for each color paint you plan to make.

4 Add food coloring to each cup until you get the color you want. Stir your paints. You're ready to paint your face. No matter how ghoulish you look, it will all come out in the wash! Have fun!

GOBLIN TRACKS

Here's how to make goblins appear—without anyone hearing the pitter-patter of their little feet.

Here's what you need:

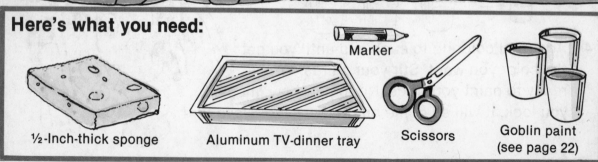

½-Inch-thick sponge   Aluminum TV-dinner tray   Scissors   Marker   Goblin paint (see page 22)

Here's what you do:

1 Use a marker to draw two feet on the sponge. You can follow the pattern shown here. Cut out the feet.

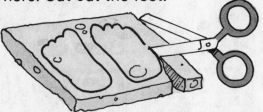

2 Make the "Goblin Paint" described on page 22. Pour the paint into an aluminum tray. The paint should be about ⅛ inch deep.

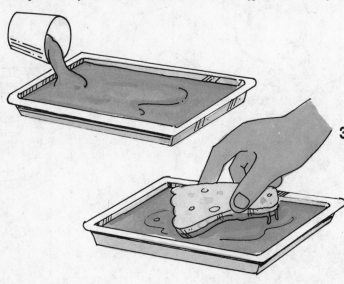

3 Dip each foot into the paint and begin printing. Remember to alternate feet as you move along!

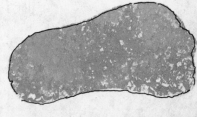

You can use these tiny tracks to decorate your own spooky writing paper. They also look good on a goblin's trick-or-treat bag!

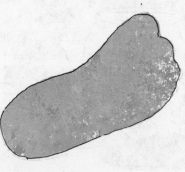

BATTY WITCH

Here's a witch costume that will drive everyone batty!

Here's what you need:

2 Yards dark cloth

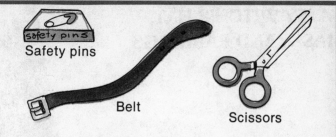

Safety pins

Belt

Scissors

Here's what you do:

1 Fold the piece of cloth in half...and in half again.

2 Cut a quarter-circle across the folded corner, as shown.

3 Open the cloth and see if your head will fit through the hole. If not, remove the cloth and enlarge the hole a little bit at a time until it fits.

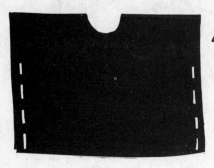

4 Lay the folded cloth down, as shown. Pin both sides closed with safety pins, leaving about 12 inches of space near the top on either side for armholes. Now turn the cloth inside out, so the pinned side faces in.

5 Your witch's dress is ready to wear. Slip it on, add a belt, and you'll look bewitching! If you have any extra material, you can add a cloak. Turn the page to find out how to make some batty accessories for your costume.

BATTY WITCH'S HAT, MASK, AND EARRINGS

Here's what you need:

2 Sheets black posterboard

Colored paper

String

Pencil

Newspapers

Scissors

Pipe cleaners

Hole puncher

Tape

Ruler

Marker

Glitter

Glue

Here's what you do to make the hat:

1 Locate point A (shown below) on a sheet of 18- by 24-inch black posterboard.

2 Tie a piece of string 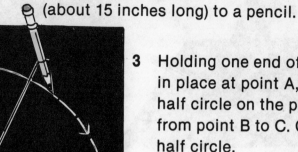 (about 15 inches long) to a pencil.

3 Holding one end of the string in place at point A, draw a half circle on the posterboard from point B to C. Cut out the half circle.

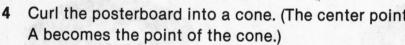

Center point A

4 Curl the posterboard into a cone. (The center point A becomes the point of the cone.)

5 Try the cone on your head. Adjust it for a snug fit.

6 Glue the cone together. Let it dry.

To find out how to make the brim of the hat, turn the page.

7 Place the cone on the other sheet of posterboard. Trace around the bottom of the cone onto the posterboard.

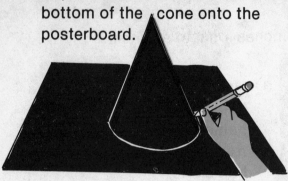

8 The line you traced is the hat line. Draw another circle about 1½ inches in from the hat line. Now draw a third circle about 3 inches beyond the hat line. This will be the brim of your hat.

9 First, cut a circle along the outer brim. Next cut out the inner circle you drew. Now snip in from the inner circle to the hat line. Make a snip about every inch all around. Then fold up the tabs.

10 Apply glue to each tab. Then put the cone over the tabs. Press the glued tabs to the cone until the glue begins to set. Allow the glue to dry completely before wearing your hat.

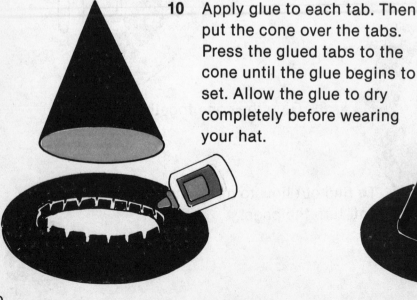

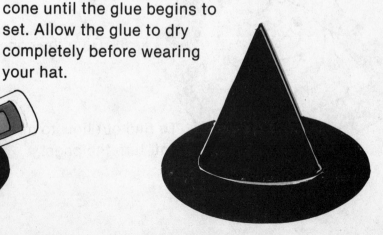

Here's what you do to make the witch's mask:

1 Copy this mask pattern onto black posterboard. Draw ovals for the eyeholes. Cut out the mask.

2 Now use a hole puncher to make two holes for the strings. Carefully cut out the eyeholes with scissors.

3 Spread newspapers over your work area. Decorate your mask by first applying glue in a bat design. Then sprinkle glitter over the glue and let it dry. Shake off the extra glitter.

4 Tie a piece of string to each hole.

**Here's what you do to make
the earrings:**

1 Cut two circles of the size shown here out of yellow construction paper.

2 Draw a spooky bat on each earring. Color it with black marker.

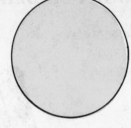

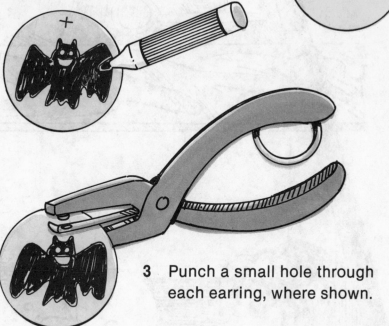

3 Punch a small hole through each earring, where shown.

4 Make a large loop at one end of a pipe cleaner. Thread the other end of the pipe cleaner through the hole in the earring and knot it. Do the same for the other earring. To wear, loop the ends of the earrings around your ears.

SPOOKY SPIDER

Here's what you need:

Black construction paper

Orange paper

Thin, black elastic

Scissors

Pencil

4 Black pipe cleaners

Glue

Here's what you do:

1 Fold a piece of black paper in half, as shown, and copy the pattern for the spider's body onto it. Cut out the shape.

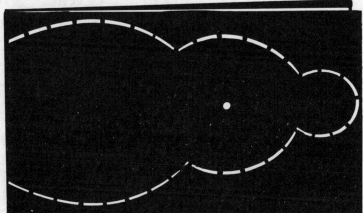

2 Open up the body shape. Spread glue over the bottom half. Then make a small hole in the top half of the body.

3 Put four pipe cleaners across the body for the spider's legs. Now thread the elastic through the hole and knot it as shown. Press the body shapes together, so the knotted end of elastic and the pipe cleaners are in between.

4 When the glue is completely dry, bend the pipe cleaners to look like legs. Cut out two circles from orange paper for eyes, and glue in place.

5 To scare everyone with your spider, just loop the end of the elastic over your finger. The spider will dance and dangle!

35

BIGFOOT MONSTER TRACKS

The mysterious Bigfoot Monster is said to live on mountains or deep in the forest. Only a few people have ever seen it. But many have seen its giant footprints. You can make mysterious giant footprints appear, too. These monster feet make great tracks in sand, mud, soft dirt, snow, or piles of wet leaves.

Here's what you need:

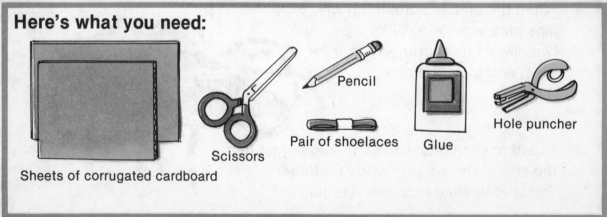

Sheets of corrugated cardboard

Scissors

Pencil

Pair of shoelaces

Glue

Hole puncher

Here's what you do:

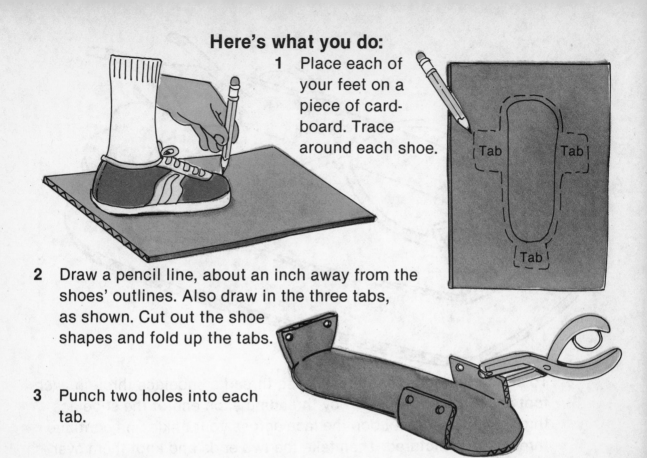

1 Place each of your feet on a piece of cardboard. Trace around each shoe.

2 Draw a pencil line, about an inch away from the shoes' outlines. Also draw in the three tabs, as shown. Cut out the shoe shapes and fold up the tabs.

3 Punch two holes into each tab.

4 Place each foot shape on a larger sheet of cardboard. Draw huge monster feet around each one. Cut out each monster-foot pattern.

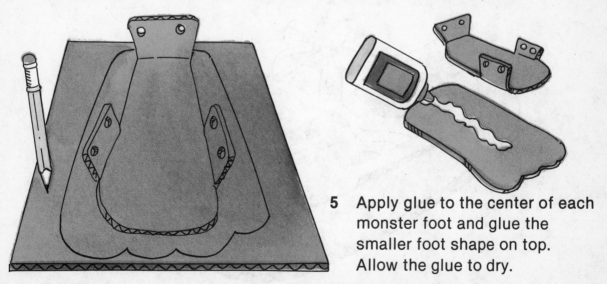

5 Apply glue to the center of each monster foot and glue the smaller foot shape on top. Allow the glue to dry.

Turn the page for more instructions.

37

6 To attach Bigfoot's feet to *your* feet, thread a shoelace through each foot shape, as shown. Start by threading each end of the shoelace through the heel tab. Loop the lace across your ankle and continue threading, as pictured. Then take the two ends and knot them over your toes.

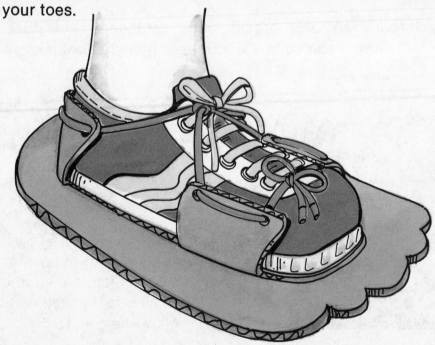

Now you're ready to leave Bigfoot's mysterious trail!

BIGFOOT MONSTER MASK

Here's what you need:

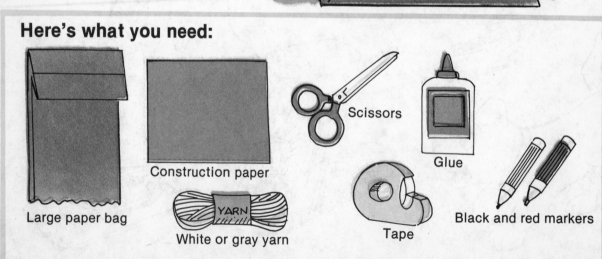

Large paper bag

White or gray yarn

Construction paper

Scissors

Tape

Glue

Black and red markers

Here's what you do:

1 Put the paper bag over your head. Carefully use a marker to mark two spots where the eye-holes will go, and a line where your mouth is.

2 Remove the bag from your head. Cut out circles for the eyes. Then cut out the opening for the mouth.

3 Copy the nose pattern shown here onto construction paper. Cut out the shape and fold along the dotted lines. Fold down the tabs and apply glue to them. Glue the nose to the bag.

4 Use a black marker to add the eyebrows. Then out-line the mouth with a red marker.

5 Cut lots of pieces of yarn into 6-inch lengths. Tape the yarn to the bag, as shown. Or—if you glue the yarn to the bag, dab the ends of the yarn into glue. When the glued end of yarn becomes tacky, firmly stick it on the bag.

FRANKENSTEIN'S MONSTER MASK

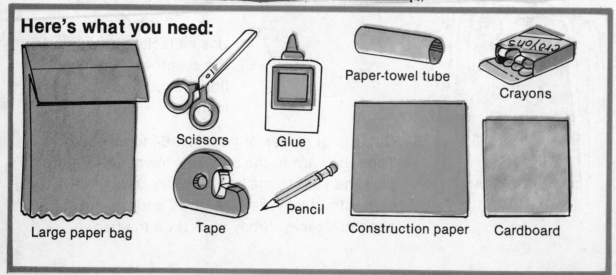

Here's what you need:

Large paper bag

Scissors

Glue

Paper-towel tube

Crayons

Tape

Pencil

Construction paper

Cardboard

42

Here's what you do:

1   Cut out the eyeholes in a paper bag, as you did for the "Bigfoot Mask" on page 40. Color the bag with green crayon. Use black crayon for the hair, mouth, eyebrows, and scar.

2   Cut a paper-towel tube into two lengths, each about 3 inches long. Make 1-inch slits around one end of each tube. Fold the tabs up, as shown.

3   On a piece of cardboard, draw a circle that is a bit larger than the hole of the tube. Cut the circle out. Draw a black line across the circle.

4   Copy the nose pattern onto construction paper. Cut out the nose, and fold the tabs along the dotted lines, as shown. Glue the tabs to the paper bag.

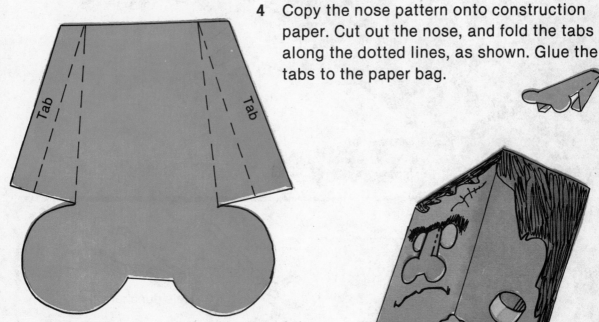

Tab   Tab

5   To finish, cut a circle, the size of the paper-towel tube, on either side of the bag. Insert the tubes in the holes and glue the tabs to the inside of the bag. Glue the circle you cut out in Step 3 to the outside of one of the tubes.

MYSTERIOUS CAT MASK

Here's what you need:

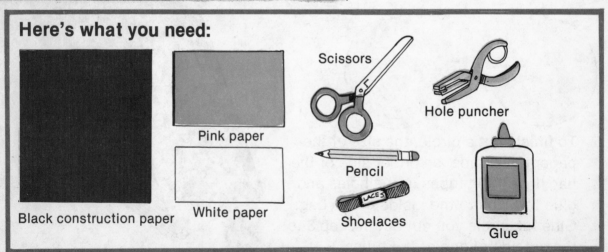

Black construction paper

Pink paper

White paper

Scissors

Pencil

Shoelaces

Hole puncher

Glue

Here's what you do:

1   Copy the mask pattern (shown on the next two pages) onto black construction paper. Cut it out. Carefully cut out the eyeholes.

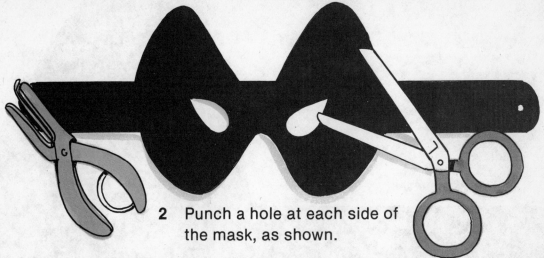

2   Punch a hole at each side of the mask, as shown.

3   Turn to pages 46-47 to find the ear and whiskers patterns. Cut out two ear shapes and two sets of whiskers.

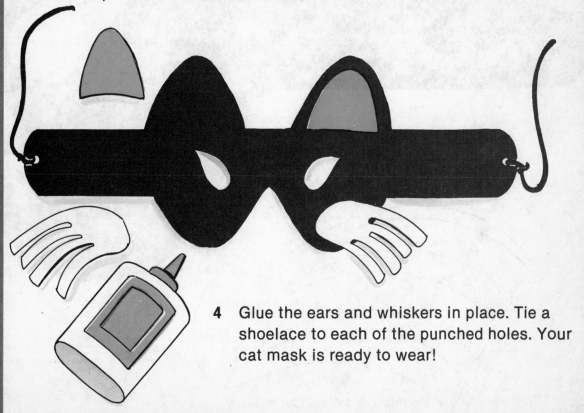

4   Glue the ears and whiskers in place. Tie a shoelace to each of the punched holes. Your cat mask is ready to wear!

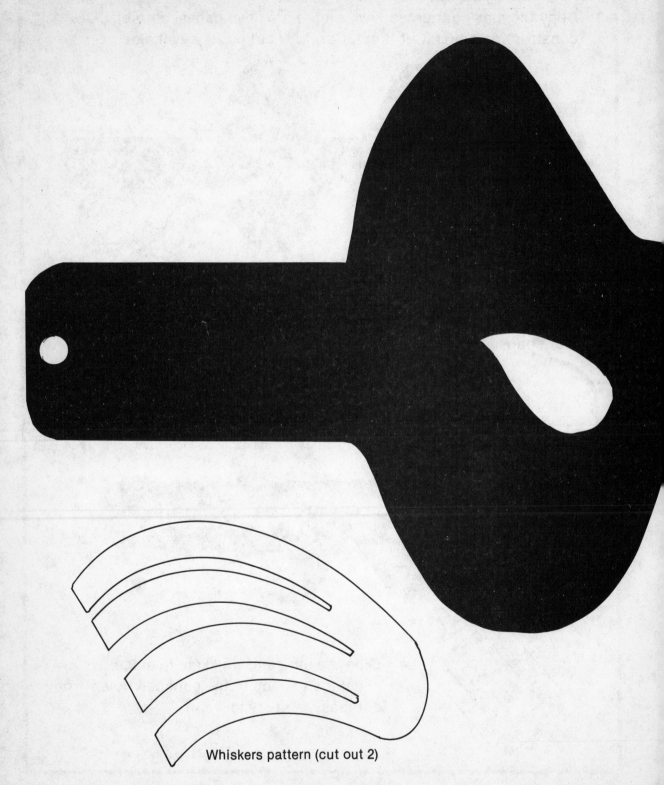

Whiskers pattern (cut out 2)